BROADWAY

The Life, Times, & Music Series

BROADWAY

The Life, Times, & Music Series

Elizabeth Rothwell

Friedman/Fairfax Publishers

A FRIEDMAN/FAIRFAX BOOK

ISBN 0-9627134-6-5

THE LIFE, TIMES,& MUSIC SERIES:BROADWAY
was prepared and produced by
Friedman/Fairfax Publishers
15 West 26th Street
New York, New York 10010

Editor: Nathaniel Marunas
Art Director: Jeff Batzli
Photography Editor: Grace How
Production Director: Karen Matsu Greenberg

Designed by Zemsky Design

Cover collage images courtesy of The Museum of the City of New York,
The Theater Collection.

Grateful acknowledgement is given to authors, publishers, and photographers for permission to reprint material. Every effort has been made to determine copyright owners of photographs and illustrations. In the case of any omissions, the Publishers will be pleased to make suitable acknowledgements in future editions.

Printed in the United States of America

ACKNOWLEDGMENTS

The author would like to thank the Columbia University Department of History for their patience and tolerance, Peter O.E. Bekker for his guidance, and Buddy Rothwell and Micah Fenhagen for their constant support and encouragement in the preparation of this manuscript.

❤❤❤❤❤❤❤❤❤❤❤❤❤❤❤❤❤❤❤❤

CONTENTS

Introduction:
Musical Theater in the
Twentieth Century

As the twentieth century wanes, the music of Broadway is being reexamined and rediscovered. Harry Connick, Jr., the popular young singer and piano player, has risen to fame as a performer of music that was popular much earlier in the century. In The Fabulous Baker Boys, Michelle Pfeiffer, Jeff Bridges, and Beau Bridges play the members of a cocktail lounge piano trio who perform a steady selection of "standards," many of which originated in Broadway shows. The opera diva Frederica von Staadt has recorded an anthology of Rodgers and Hart songs called My Funny Valentine with the London Symphony Orchestra. Singers and songwriters such as Linda Ronstadt, Carly Simon, and Willie Nelson have all recorded albums of standards, dusting off old tunes for the ears of a new generation.

A revival of Guys and Dolls, *the quintessential Broadway musical, swept the Tony Awards in 1992.*

On Broadway itself, revivals are busting out all over. There have been restagings of *Sweet Charity, Me and My Girl, The Most Happy Fella, Man of La Mancha, Anything Goes,* and *Guys and Dolls.* Tributes to Broadway's history are also the rage, with retrospective productions such as *The Will Rogers Follies, My One and Only,* and *Crazy For You.*

Musical theater is a distinctly American art form. The collaborative process involving composers, lyricists, playwrights, choreographers, performers, directors, and designers parallels the melting pot of cultural influences that came together to form the nation itself. One of Broadway's longest running musicals, *A Chorus Line,* placed mirrors along the back of the stage in which the audience could see itself. This is the metaphor of Broadway. Behind the chorus line, we find ourselves and our experiences.

The tradition and institution that we know as Broadway slowly came together. The gut appeal of show tunes ripens to deep appreciation when the music is heard as part of an unfolding story that leads from minstrel show to vaudeville, from operetta to stage spectacle, from burlesque to musical comedy—and finally to the Broadway musical as we know it today.

Buddy Ebsen and Colette Lyons in Showboat *at the Trocadero Theater.*

The Birth of Broadway– Operas and Operettas

Operettas were a major component in the development of the Broadway musical and dominated the market throughout the first decades of this century. As a European import, the operettas Americans saw had a history of cross-cultural and multinational evolution that dated back to a revolt against the aristocratic grand opera in the late eighteenth and early nineteenth centuries. In the latter century, opera began to be performed and seen by the middle class, and they started fashioning it to their own uses.

Operetta, light opera, opéra comique, comic opera, opéra bouffe, and *opera buffa* are all forms of popular opera. Confusingly, opéra comique is not the same as comic opera, light opera is not the same as operetta, and opera bouffe is not simply the French form of Italian opera buffa. Technically, they are all stories told through music with accompanying dialogue–a characterization that also defines Broadway musicals. On paper, the distinctions among them are vague, but on stage, each of the forms has an obviously different style.

Opera buffa ("buffa" is of the same root as "buffoon") first appeared in Italy in the seventeenth century in the form of short *intermezzo* (intermission) entertainments that would take place before the curtain during scene changes. These short pieces were immensely popular and grew into full-length pieces, with

Jacques Offenbach (1819-1880).

Johann Strauss' Die Fledermaus, *nearly 120 years old, is still performed today.*

audiences of their own. Opera buffa contrasted grand opera by focusing on themes that related to the day-to-day lives of people, rather than on the remote classical themes that informed grand opera. Although to modern ears its sound may blur into grand opera, opera buffa was very distinct to eighteenth-century audiences.

When the new Italian opera buffa was heard in France, it was eagerly adopted by the Parisian Opéra-Comique, which opened in 1715. In France, opéra bouffe referred to music-hall and vaudeville shows, so the term "comique" was adopted instead of the more logical "bouffe"; nonetheless, opéra comique was much the same as Italian buffa. Touchy about the incursion on grand opera, the

The ornate Niblo's Theater in New York, c. 1865.

Académie de Musique took legal action against the Opéra-Comique that required dialogue to be spoken in opéra comique in order to plainly distinguish it from "real" opera. (This scenario would be replayed in New York in the twentieth century when the Metropolitan Opera Company paid Oscar Hammerstein, Sr. a reported $1,000,000 in 1909 to shut down his shiny new Manhattan Opera Company.)

W.S. Gilbert wrote the lyrics...

The invention of the piano in 1711 had a tremendous influence upon the spread of popular opera. Providing a relatively inexpensive, full-bodied, and informal accompaniment to singing, the piano allowed popular opera to reach a much larger audience.

By the middle of the nineteenth century, however, the classical orientation of opéra comique began to seem a little dull. In 1859, a cellist in the orchestra of

Offenbach's last work, The Tales of Hoffman, *Metropolitan Opera House, 1880.*

the Opéra-Comique, Jacques Offenbach (1819–1880), rented out the tiny Théâtre des Bouffes-Parisiens and staged the premiere of his operetta *Orfée aux Enfers*. Universally loathed by the critics, *Orfée aux Enfers* was a smash-hit parody of Gluck's classical opera *Orpheus and Eurydice* (1762).

Offenbach's lively and melodic scores incorporated all the latest developments in music—waltzes, marches, and even the can-can, which was considered indecent. (The can-can seems today to be a quintessentially Parisian motif, but it was in fact a North African import.)

Offenbach's treatment of the myth of Orpheus resembles a "Fractured Fairy Tale" from the *Rocky and Bullwinkle* TV show. Orpheus, who has a voice so

... And Arthur Sullivan wrote the music.

beautiful that it hypnotizes the guardians of hell, in Offenbach's hands became an intolerably narcissistic violin player. When Orpheus descends to the Underworld to rescue Eurydice, she prefers staying there to going with him.

Not to be outdone by the Parisians, a composer named Franz von Suppe wrote the first Viennese operetta, which opened in November 1860. The Viennese waltz, with its shimmering hesitation, proved to be a perfect frame for the new opera form. Johann Strauss (1825–1899), the "King of the Waltz," became the "Emperor of Operetta" with his first attempt, *Indigo and the Forty Thieves*, in 1870. His classic *Die Fledermaus* appeared in 1874.

The continent was soon overrun with operettas. Touring from country to country, hundreds upon hundreds of new works were produced throughout the remainder of the ninteenth century. Offenbach himself was won over by the Viennese and wrote over 100 works that he classified as operetta. His last work, *The Tales of Hoffman*, was produced three months after his death in 1880. Strauss wrote only eleven operattas, but they are universally considered the finest and most enduring in the genre. He died in 1899 as the result of a cold he caught while conducting a gala revival of *Die Fledermaus*.

Opposite page: Ethel Merman as Reno Sweeney in Cole Porter's Anything Goes, *1934.*

In England, the late-nineteenth-century form of popular opera arose not out of music but out of poetry. *Light verse* was a popular, highly organized form involving absolute command of complicated internal rhyme schemes, obscure allusionary metrical patterns, and a viciously cynical sense of humor.

W. S. Gilbert (1836–1911) excelled at it. A not-so-brilliant lawyer, Gilbert began collaborating in 1875 with a very good composer, Arthur Sullivan (1842–1900), and light verse became light opera. Because their success was based more on Gilbert's clever and totally untranslatable lyrics than on Sullivan's music, Gilbert and Sullivan never had much of a following across the English Channel. Or perhaps since many of their plots involved merciless parodies of French and Viennese operetta, their cousins on the continent pretended not to understand. However, this sort of badinage did appeal to audiences in the United States, where Gilbert and Sullivan shows continue to enjoy immense popularity to this day.

A Portrait of the Art Form as a Leggy Young Lady

In 1866, a Parisian ballet troupe lost its booking when the New York City theater where it was performing burned down. Desperate for money, the troupe was snatched up by an ingenious producer who put them in his eye-popping new play, *The Black Crook*. With elaborate scenery, *The Black Crook* ran over five hours, entrancing audiences with its miraculous transformations of grand staircases into fairy grottos and then into mid-ocean storms. While spectacular scene changes had been a theatrical tradition dating back to the French royal court of Louis XIV, *The*

The Broadway formula was an accidental discovery with The Black Crook *in 1886.*

Black Crook used the most modern technology available to achieve an undreamed-of realism. All that flash and dazzle sold tickets. And the ballet troupe provided another scenic element that also contributed to higher box office draws: female legs.

Despite the precedent of *The Black Crook*, American musical entertainment remained stratified throughout the 1800s. There was burlesque and vaudeville, opera and operetta, music halls and minstrel shows, ragtime and romance—each appealing to a particular segment of society. But as segmented immigrant populations began increasingly to interact, the many popular forms of entertainment likewise began to coalesce.

Sheet music for the "Amazon's March" from The Black Crook.

Early Broadway:
Operetta and Musical Comedy

In the first decades of the twentieth century, Broadway theaters offered only two kinds of entertainment: operetta and musical comedy. Operettas were a European import. Musical comedies had no plots—they were simply disconnected revues of music and comedy.

The word "vaudeville" comes from the French "Vau-de-Vire," a region in Normandy known for its lovely song. In the United States, "vaudeville" more readily evokes images of loud men in funny suits. Traditionally, vaudevillians were traveling entertainers who were unable to invest time or money in developing full-length productions. They were hired by tavern owners to draw a crowd, and their shows required no plot or scenery, just some gags and music. Ultimately, this itinerant style found a home in New York City—where there were plenty of taverns—and made a lasting mark.

Irish vaudevillians Harrigan and Hart explored international relations in Ireland vs. Italy.

In 1879, two Irish comics named Ned Harrigan (1845–1911) and Tony Hart (1855–1891) opened a theater at Broadway and Spring Street in New York with *The Mulligan Guards' Ball*. The adventures continued with *The Mulligan Guards' Christmas*, *The Mulligan Guards' Surprise*, and other comic explorations of the lives of the Irish working class in New York. By using Irish stereotypes (drunks and cops for the most part) in the lead roles, Harrigan and Hart became heroes to the enormous Irish immigrant population. As the Irish gained their footing, however, they left the Mulligan Guards behind. Out of business by 1900, Ned Harrigan was nevertheless immortalized in George M. Cohan's "H-A-double-R-I (G-A-N Spells HARRIGAN)" from the 1908 production of *An American Idea*.

As the tide of Irish immigrants ebbed, the Jewish tide flowed. In 1896, four years after Ellis Island was opened as an immigrant clearing house in New York Harbor, Joe Weber (1867–1942) and Lew Fields (1867–1941) opened their music hall on Twenty-ninth Street and Broadway. Former employees of the Harlem Opera House, owned by Oscar Hammerstein, Sr. (1846–1919), Weber and Fields were masters of burlesque—farcical reenactments of serious dramatic works. Borrowing the plot of whatever drama was playing up the street on Broadway, Weber and Fields created their own peculiar brand of absurd, Yiddish-accented operetta parody. Zany, fast, and full of purposeful misunderstandings, their work was a genre

George M. Cohan (left) shares the stage with his family.

The scandalous "Florodora Sextette," Broadway's first chorus line, 1900.

unto itself. Their music hall ran successfully until 1902, and then broke apart because of a personality conflict: they just couldn't stand each other. Lew Fields continued to produce musical comedy, and Joe Weber later appeared in operettas on Broadway. Their style was revived and immortalized on film a generation later by the Marx Brothers.

The teams of Harrigan and Hart and of Weber and Fields reflected the similar but separate struggles of Irish and Jewish immigrants. While Harrigan and Hart's foil was the difficulty of maintaining Irishness on American soil, Weber and Fields explored the mayhem that ensued from trying to translate American culture

into the Yiddish idiom. While both teams dealt with stereotypes, each had the luxury of stereotyping its own ethnic group.

For African-Americans, however, this issue had an entirely different meaning. Entertainment, like nearly everything else in the country at the time, was racially segregated. While minstrel shows were a popular form of entertainment in the nineteenth century, they were not an African-American entertainment. In fact, they often involved cruel parodies of African-Americans with white performers in "blackface" makeup. After the Civil War, some blacks performed in minstrel shows, but they too wore blackface. Minstrel shows died before the turn of the century, but blackface stuck around a good deal longer. African-Americans and blackface

Sheet music from George M. Cohan's Little Johnny Jones.

characters were prohibited from interacting onstage with white performers. Harrigan and Hart's use of performers in blackface was considered scandalous.

In 1900, William McKinley was reelected president, women did not yet have the right to vote, Sigmund Freud published *The Interpretation of Dreams*, and an operetta named *Florodora*, an import from the British Gaiety Theatre, opened on Broadway. Partially set in the exotic Philippines, which had become a U.S. territory only two years earlier, the American rendition featured six talented actresses singing "Tell Me Pretty Maiden" in the second act. The "Florodora Sextette" were the rage of New York: an operetta chorus with music-hall mannerisms, they winked audaciously at favored audience members.

Florodora became the first Broadway production of the twentieth century to catapult the hit-show hurdle and run for five hundred performances. The Sextette had a high turnover as various members fell into the arms of wealthy stage-door admirers who showered them with champagne, flowers, jewelry, and stock-market tips. Evelyn Nesbitt, a later member of the cast, achieved her greatest fame as the beauty whose jealous husband shot the architect Stanford White at Madison Square Garden in 1906.

The success of *Florodora*, with a wink to the audience, was the first indication of the money to be made in breaking down class barriers on the musical stage. It was a short skip-step from *Florodora* to Florenz Ziegfeld, who improved on the concept of flirtatious operetta girls by dispensing with the operetta.

Florenz Ziegfeld

Employing hundreds of people, Ziegfeld (1869–1932) annually produced his spectacular *Follies* from 1907 to 1931. He sought an audience with money in its pocket, and captured it by satisfying the newly risen middle class with his unique brand of entertainment. Drawing upon the French tradition of *Folies*—literally, "madness"—the *Ziegfeld Follies* were lavishly designed and orchestrated vaudeville revues with winning combinations of music, dancing, and comedy. In Ziegfeld's hands, a fourth element was introduced: spectacle.

Above: Florenz Ziegfeld. Right: The impressive facade of the Ziegfeld Theater.

The Hippodrome

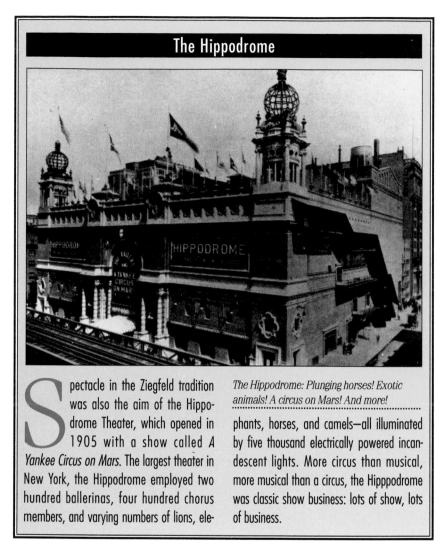

Spectacle in the Ziegfeld tradition was also the aim of the Hippodrome Theater, which opened in 1905 with a show called *A Yankee Circus on Mars.* The largest theater in New York, the Hippodrome employed two hundred ballerinas, four hundred chorus members, and varying numbers of lions, ele-

The Hippodrome: Plunging horses! Exotic animals! A circus on Mars! And more!

phants, horses, and camels—all illuminated by five thousand electrically powered incandescent lights. More circus than musical, more musical than a circus, the Hipppodrome was classic show business: lots of show, lots of business.

The *Follies* exemplified the new American style of the twentieth century. The set designs by Joseph Urban (1872-1933) were startling, sumptuous, and modern; the costumes were outrageous.

Ziegfeld bought the best of everything: the best composers, the best designers, the best singers, the best comedians, the best musicians. A relentless self-promoter, he wanted the best not because of a sensitive regard for a fledgling American art form, but because he wisely understood that the best would always sell. The list of writers and composers on the Ziegfeld payroll reads like a Who's Who of early-twentieth-century American music: Jerome Kern (1885–1945), Irving Berlin (1888–1989), Vincent Youmans (1898–1946), Sigmund Romberg (1887–1951), and Harold Arlen (1905-1946).

Parading pristinely, the Ziegfeld Girls represented all the glorious virtues of The American Girl. They often disappointed Ziegfeld by behaving scandalously offstage, but with a willing suspension of disbelief, the chorus line was raised in the public imagination to an acceptable level of respectability.

Publicity shot of Marjorie Chapin, a Ziegfeld Girl who was rumored to be engaged to "an Indian Rajah."

Irving Berlin

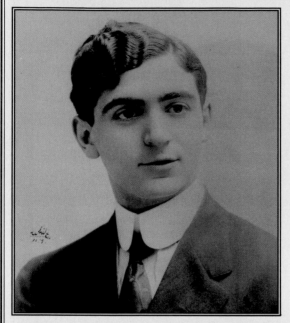

A n icon of the musical theater, Irving Berlin was born in Siberia in 1888. He came with his parents to New York City at the age of four, three years before his father died. Berlin was forced from an early age to struggle for money, and found various jobs working as a paper boy, singing waiter, and so on.

Finding his way into Tin Pan Alley as a song plugger, he published his first song at nineteen and had his first big hit, "Alexander's Ragtime Band," in 1911. His first Broadway show, *Watch Your Step*, was staged in 1914; he would write four more shows before going to work for Ziegfeld in 1919.

By 1921, Berlin was able to buy his own theater, The Music Box, on West Forty-sixth Street, where he staged a series called *The Music Box Revue* through 1924. Thematic but plotless—and featuring plenty of women—*The Music Box Revue* was the staged equivalent of music video.

Berlin's main concern was getting music before the public. His "book musicals," although few and far between, were

Berlin joins the war effort with "This is the Army," 1942.

Annie Get Your Gun *was made-to-order for Ethel Merman, 1946.*

composed primarily as vehicles for the performers: *The Cocoanuts* (1925) for the Marx Brothers, with George S. Kaufman, and *Annie Get Your Gun* (1946) for Ethel Merman.

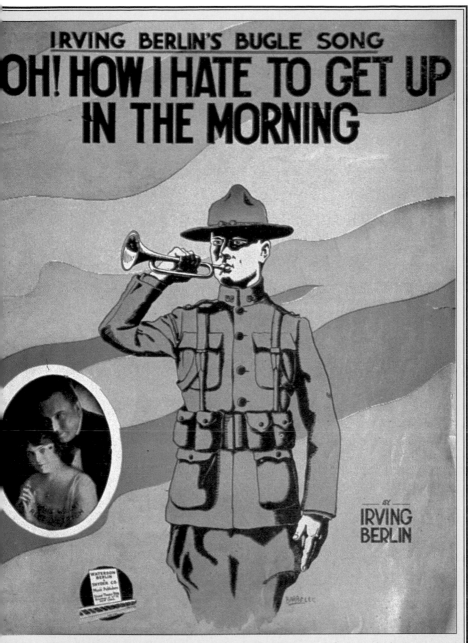

The sale of sheet music was serious business and the true measure of a songwriter's success.

Above all else a songwriter, Berlin is known less for his shows than for his songs: "White Christmas," "Let's Have Another Cup O' Coffee," "God Bless America," "Puttin' on the Ritz," "Oh! How I Hate to Get Up in the Morning," "Have Yourself a Merry Little Christmas," "Blue Skies," and "There's No Business Like Show Business," to name only a few.

Once discovered, Berlin never again worried about work or money. He hired assistants to transcribe and score his music. Berlin had no formal musical training—he could barely play a piano—and his incomprehensibly large catalog was composed entirely in the key of F-sharp, using only the black keys. In addition, he purchased a piano fitted with a special mechanism that could shift the tuning so he could play in any key without having to touch the white ones.

The Princess Theater

Between 1915 and 1920, a series of stylish shows were performed at the Princess Theater, a piece of property on West Thirty-ninth Street in New York formerly owned by Jake Shubert. Because it was so small—only 299 seats—nobody knew what to do with it. At the suggestion of a producer, composer Jerome Kern and playwright Guy Bolton (1884–1979) began an adaptation of an English play called *Mr. Popple of Ippleton*. Sensing that the title might not sell, Bolton renamed it *Nobody Home*, and wrote lyrics for Kern's score. Although not a huge success, it attracted attention, and the Princess became a going concern.

On the opening night of their second show, *Very Good Eddie*, Kern and Bolton approached the English novelist P. G. Wodehouse (1881–1975), who was in the audience. When he was reluctant to comment on the quality of the show's lyrics, he was drafted to take over the job of lyricist himself. The Kern-Bolton-Wodehouse collaboration thrived for six productions and broke off only when Wodehouse was obliged to return to his Jeeves novels.

The collaboration had a strong British current, with just enough American grounding to connect with its New York audience. Kern was the son of a well-to-do New York family—he was named for the Jerome House on Jerome Avenue where he was born, in a privileged section of the Bronx—but he had spent his early career in London. Guy Bolton had an international upbringing: born to American parents in London, he was educated in Brooklyn and Paris. P. G. Wodehouse was just plain British through and through.

The Princess shows were a sophisticated development for the New York stage. Scaled to the small house, the shows focused on the plays as much as the music, and in the British tradition of Gilbert and Sullivan, also relied heavily on wit.

Top: The Princess Theater was the home of a sophisticated shift of sensibility, 1915-1920. Above: The second Kern-Bolton collaboration for the Princess Theater.

The extremely popular Bert Williams was the only black comedian to appear in the *Follies*. Although he was never permitted onstage at the same time as the Ziegfeld Girls, and was never invited to appear in the *Follies* movies, his name was as well-known as that of his costar W. C. Fields.

The *Follies* were the toast of vaudeville. After Ziegfeld, the homey, lighthearted, neighborhood entertainment began to look a little flat.

In 1912, Jake Shubert (1878–1963) bcgan a Zicgfcld-like series called *Passing Shows*, which ran annually through 1924 in the Shubert family's Winter Garden theater. In 1923 and 1924 the Shuberts would also stage a short-lived series called *Artists and Models*, which featured tititlatingly tasteful and artistic nudity. The Shubert family owned many theaters, and protected their interests by producing the shows themselves. They also employed Sigmund Romberg as a staff composer, pressing him into service for whatever project was at hand. These projects included showcases of the super-popular

Although he was a star of the Ziegfeld Follies, *Bert Williams had to appear alone onstage because he was black.*

Oscar Hammerstein II

Steered away from the theater and into Columbia University by his family, Hammerstein nevertheless discovered varsity shows there and dropped out of law school. In 1920, he wrote his first hit, *Tickle Me*, in collaboration with lyricist Otto Harbach (1873–1963). He continued to work with Harbach throughout the 1920s, although he did write for other composers as well (Sigmund Romberg, for instance, with whom he created *The Desert Song* in 1926).

The librettist Oscar Hammerstein II (1895–1960) was the grandson of Oscar Hammerstein, an opera impresario, and the son of Willie Hammerstein, a vaudeville producer. Born in Harlem in 1895, his full name was Oscar Greeley Clendenning Hammerstein. He chose the "II" mostly to distinguish himself from his operatic grandfather.

Hammerstein had a long and prosperous career, his biggest contributions coming during his collaboration with Richard Rodgers (1902–1975) in the 1940s and 1950s. Rodgers and Hammerstein wrote, among other Broadway shows, *Oklahoma!*, *Carousel*, *South Pacific*, *The King and I*, and *The Sound of Music* (which starred Mary Martin in the U. S. production).

Top: Oscar Hammerstein II (left), with Jerome Kern.
Above: Yul Brynner and Gertrude Lawrence in The King and I, *1951.*

Al Jolson (1889-1950) at the Winter Garden in the late 1920s, where Romberg's talents went somewhat unappreciated. (Jolson often revised the score midway through the show, and even sent the cast home as the spirit moved him to a solo performance.)

George White, a former Ziegfeld tap dancer, also had his hoof in the revue circles, with a light and fast series called *Scandals*, which ran from 1919 to

Tin Pan Alley

Tin Pan Alley was the nickname given to the stretch of New York City's West Twenty-eighth Street where music publishers kept their offices. In order to sell their sheet music, usually at a nickel a pop, the publishers hired piano players to "plug" the tunes for customers who dropped by.

Song pluggers had to be versatile; they had to sell music of all styles to people of all inclinations. "The Alley" may have gotten its name when one plugger selling a song for guitar put sheets of paper behind the strings to get his piano to sound more like the real thing: a reporter wrote that the result sounded more like a tin pan.

1931. George White used the music of George Gershwin (1898–1937) for his shows. *Vanities* was another revue, slightly smuttier than the others, produced by Earl Carroll (1893–1948) from 1923 to 1933.

The reign of the American operetta was a period of awkward struggle as composers, many of them born and trained in Europe, tried to keep American audiences interested in the form. Usually set in faraway, long-ago, or mythical

locations, composed of endless waltzes and marches, operettas had plots that always seemed to be resolved by an unspoiled young soprano who, at long last, was romantically united with a dashing young tenor in military uniform.

The operetta served its purpose for a while, but a country recently freed from the grasp of faraway lands simply didn't want the same old European brand of entertainment, anymore than it wanted to hear incessant waltzing and marching.

Costume design for Carousel, *1945.*

Broadway's Ship Comes In

In 1927, *Showboat* arrived.

Girded by Jerome Kern's success with the Princess Theater shows—and probably not hurt by Oscar Hammerstein II's family connections—Kern and Hammerstein sold Ziegfeld on producing a Broadway show based on an American novel.

Backed by Ziegfeld and all that he commanded—an unerring eye, sets by Joseph Urban, the immense stage of the Ziegfeld Theater, and more—*Showboat* changed the course of Broadway overnight. The integration of a dramatic, epic plot with music and dance had never been attempted on such a scale. The result was astonishingly successful.

The original 1927 production of Showboat.

Kern and Hammerstein, deeply aware of the risk involved, did not use a director, but, in collaboration with Ziegfeld, oversaw every aspect of the production themselves. With a plot hinging on the ruination of a biracial marriage, set sprawlingly over three generations on a Mississippi riverboat, at a Chicago fair, in a music hall, and in a convent school, *Showboat* brought unexpected realism and poignancy to the musical stage.

The characterizations in *Showboat* are virulently stereotyped. Segregation is the underlying conflict in the story, which depicts the race relations of a riverboat show company. The leading characters are all white, while the chorus is the collective voice of the black laborers who work on the showboat. The explicit

Norma Terns and Howard Marsh as Magnolia and Gaylord in a 1927 production of Showboat.

racial incident occurs when Julie LaVerne, a mulatto star of the riverboat *Cotton Blossom*, is "exposed" and forced to leave the boat with her white lover, Steve. This circumstance implicitly overshadows the relationship of Gaylord Ravenal and Magnolia Hawkes, who step in to take over Julie and Steve's roles in the Blossom revue and fall in love.

Gaylord and Magnolia's story would be operetta, but perfect romance is, in the end, only "make believe." Thus, Gaylord's compulsive gambling destroys their lives. The play concludes with Kim, the daughter of Gaylord and Magnolia, returning to the *Cotton Blossom* to appear onstage. "Ol' Man River" is the soul of *Showboat*, the final spiritual comment. Offering no answers, set apart from the drama, the black deckhand Joe is the man through whose eyes the story is seen, giving life to the sharp contrast between black labor and white play on the river.

Jerome Kern returned to the operetta form after *Showboat*, most success-fully with *Roberta*, for which he composed "Smoke Gets in Your Eyes" (lyrics by Otto Harbach) in 1933. Oscar Hammerstein continued to explore conflicts of race,

A young Ethel Merman appeared in the 1930 production of George and Ira Gershwin's Girl Crazy. *Her rendition of "I Got Rhythm" made her a star.*

class, and addiction in *South Pacific, Carousel,* and *The King and I.*

With the onset of the Depression, Broadway was forced to scale down production costs, prompting a new artistic energy. The music, book, and lyrics had to compensate for the draw of 1920s extravagance. Both Ira and George Gershwin and Rodgers and Hart collaborated with Guy Bolton for the 1930 season—the Gershwins' *Girl Crazy* appeared with the songs "Embraceable You" and "I Got Rhythm," while Rodgers and Hart put out *Simple Simon,* which included "Ten Cents A Dance."

In 1931, *Of Thee I Sing* won the Pulitzer Prize. Morrie Ryskind (1895-1985) and Ira Gershwin shared the honors for their satirical libretto about a presidential campaign. George Gershwin was left out; there was no category for music in drama.

Rodgers and Hart maintained a steady output of clever and stylish shows throughout the 1930s. Their dream of producing Princess-like shows was achieved—and surpassed. Their sensibility was grittier than that of the Kern-Bolton-Wodehouse team. In addition, Hart's lyrics, a collision of wrenching pain and loony rhyme, contained a sly wit cozier to American ears than Wodehouse's sparkling, letter-perfect drollery. Rodgers and Hart were masters of parody, especially when going after the perky fraudulence of musical comedy. Their constant presence on Broadway was a steadying force on the changing seas of show business.

Between 1925 and 1935, Broadway underwent a remarkable change. *No, No, Nanette!*'s relentlessly perky "I Want To Be Happy" had been forever outdated by Cole Porter's swank and spicy "Just One of Those Things."

Pal Joey was Rodgers and Hart's masterpiece. Based on a book by John O'Hara, who staged the play with Rodgers and Hart, this show was also Broadway's second dramatic turning point. Darker than anything that had ever

Richard Rodgers & Lorenz Hart

Richard Rodgers and Lorenz Hart produced an average of one new show every year between 1920 and 1943, the year of Hart's death.

The team met as camp counselors in 1917. Hart was several years older than Rodgers. A Columbia graduate, he was proficient in German and got a job translating operettas for the Shubert organization. Both were avid fans of Jerome Kern and his Princess Theater shows and they started an instant collaboration. They began as an amateur operation; their first shows were staged by the Columbia University Varsity Players.

The team didn't stay amateur for long. A friendship with Herbert Fields, the son of vaudeville star and producer Lew Fields, helped them supply their first Broadway contribution: one song in *Little Ritz Girl* (1920). In 1924 they put together *Melody Man*, for which Herbert Fields wrote the book. By 1930, fifteen Rodgers and Hart shows had appeared on Broadway.

Lorenz Hart was a haunted man. Just under five feet tall, he suffered constant insecurity about his appearance. Always a heavy drinker, even as early as his twenties, he often couldn't function before noon. As success grew, he sank fully into alcoholism. As he deteriorated into the final stages of alcoholism, Hart behaved more and more erratically, which became intolerable to Richard Rodgers. Rodgers forced Hart into a hospital to dry out, and installed a piano in the room next door. Hart was banned from the rehearsals of the 1943 revival of *A Connecticut Yankee in King Arthur's Court*, and was escorted from the theater on opening night. He died later that year.

Richard Rodgers (left) and Lorenz Hart.

The 1940 production of Pal Joey *made a star of Gene Kelly.*

appeared on Broadway, *Pal Joey* delved into the exploits of a manipulative, womanizing nightclub hanger-on, demonstrating his utter incapacity for change. The story did not have a happy ending; it was a musical with a leading man who makes only selfish choices and, stuck with the consequences, learns nothing. Broadway audiences were shocked that a musical would (or could) explore character in such a way. Gene Kelly, the smoothie who played Joey, became a star. The 1940 production was evidently too unusual to run longer than 374 performances, but *Pal Joey* was revived with commercial success in 1952, and a sanitized version, with Frank Sinatra playing the lead, was filmed in 1957.

George and Ira Gershwin

George Gershwin heard Irving Berlin's "Alexander's Ragtime Band" as a child of thirteen. Five years later he published his first song, "When You Want 'Em, You Can't Get 'Em, When You Get 'Em, You Don't Want 'Em." Fortunately for American music, his brother Ira soon began collaborating on all his lyrics.

Following in the footsteps of his hero, Irving Berlin, George Gershwin worked for a while as a song plugger. Not too much later Berlin himself offered Gershwin a job as his music secretary. Sensibly, Gershwin declined, going to work instead for a publisher who promised more money.

George Gershwin was born in Brooklyn in 1898, and raised on the East Side of Manhattan in a comfortable middle class family. The family's piano was purchased for his more scholarly older brother, Ira (1896–1983). George was thought to be too rowdy to settle down and learn how to play, but he astonished everyone at the age of ten by playing without having taken a single lesson.

Ira was a perfect lyricist for George. A City College dropout, Ira Gershwin had a love of language that equaled his brother's love of jazz. Ira disdained work, preferring crossword puzzles and cigars. He was happy to jump on the Broadway bandwagon, where he could indulge in the above-mentioned vices to his heart's content.

George Gershwin is often referred to as a "jazz composer," but that characterization is technically incorrect. Jazz is a performance style that depends on spontaneous improvisation of rhythm and tone. Gershwin's music drew upon jazz, but it was entirely *composed*—not improvised.

George Gershwin met Fred Astaire in 1919. Astaire would be more collaborator than interpreter to Gershwin; in 1924, when the Gershwin brothers presented their first

The Gershwin brothers: George (left) and Ira.

complete score on Broadway, Fred and his sister Adele were the stars. The book for *Lady Be Good* was written by Fred Thompson and Guy Bolton, and debuted the now classic song, "Fascinating Rhythm."

Gershwin's orchestral works such as *Rhapsody in Blue* and *Concerto in F* have never been fully accepted by the classical musical world, but *Porgy and Bess*, presented on Broadway in 1937, was later adopted into the repertoire of the Metropolitan Opera Company. In 1937, George Gershwin suffered a sudden attack, and was unable to complete a passage during a performance of his own work. Five months later, he died of a brain tumor at the age of thirty-eight.

Ira spent the rest of his days in Holly- wood, venturing out only occasionally to collaborate with Jerome Kern, Harold Arlen, and Kurt Weill.

Top: Morrie Ryskind and Ira Gershwin's prompt book from the Pulitzer-winning Of Thee I Sing, 1931. Above: Fred Astaire and his sister Adele were the original Gershwin interpreters.

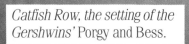

Catfish Row, the setting of the Gershwins' Porgy and Bess.

The Dream Ballet

Following Hart's death in 1943, Rodgers began a collaboration with Oscar Hammerstein and together they developed the definitive Broadway form. After *Pal Joey*, only one element remained unexplored in musical theater: dance. Rodgers and Hammerstein remedied this almost immediately in *Oklahoma!* Rodgers and Hart had

used dance before in *On Your Toes* and *Babes In Arms*, which were choreographed by George Balanchine (1904-1983). But the dream ballet in *Oklahoma!*, choreographed by Agnes de Mille (1905-), opened a new consciousness of the capacity of dance to develop character and plot in a musical setting.

Top: Rodgers and Hammerstein. Opposite page: Poster from the 1943 production of Oklahoma! *Left: Choreographer Agnes de Mille.*

Broadway in the Fifties: On the Street Where You Live...

During World War II, Broadway focused on patriotism and reverted to a Romberg-like operetta in *Song Of Norway*, an adaptation of composer Edvard Grieg's music. But in 1946, beginning with *Annie Get Your Gun* and a lavish revival of *Showboat*, the range of subject matter in musicals expanded.

In *Finian's Rainbow*, E. Y. Harburg, collaborating on book and lyrics with Fred Saidy, intertwined two stories that separately could not have sold, but together had pizzazz. One story is of a leprechaun searching for his stolen pot of gold; the other is of an Irish immigrant's entanglement in the corruption and racism of southern politics. There is a further subplot of love thwarted by a labor struggle. The plaintive "How Are Things in Glocca Morra?" is the best-known song from this show. A film version of *Finian's Rainbow* was directed by the young Francis Ford Coppola in 1968, with Fred Astaire and Petula Clark in the lead roles.

The unstoppable Richard Rodgers and the supremely dedicated Oscar Hammerstein took on the war in the South Pacific in 1949. Adapting a series of James Michener short stories in collaboration with Joshua Logan, Rodgers and Hammerstein wrote *South Pacific* with Mary Martin and the opera

Mary Martin as Ensign Nellie Forbush in South Pacific.

In 1949, South Pacific *examined the role of women in the military.*

star Ezio Pinza in mind. Pinza's crossover from the Metropolitan Opera to the Broadway stage represented a cultural landmark in itself. His operatic rendition of "Some Enchanted Evening" was considered a tour de force.

Like *Showboat, South Pacific* also explored racial prejudice. With a plot that revolved around two interracial affairs, *South Pacific* ran for an amazing 1,925 performances. Mary Martin shampooed her hair onstage at least that many times singing, "I'm Gonna Wash That Man Right Outta My Hair." Mitzi Gaynor was hired for the 1958 film, but Mary Martin remains in the minds of many as the original Ensign Nellie Forbush.

Irving Berlin was still a presence on Broadway in 1949. With book by playwright Robert E. Sherwood, music and lyrics by Irving Berlin, direction by Moss Hart, and choreography by Jerome Robbins, *Miss Liberty* was an inexplicable flop. Running for only 308 shows, it was the story of an American in Paris who mistakes a French girl for the model who posed for the Statue of Liberty. It seems that postwar audiences were in no mood for "An Old-Fashioned Walk."

More to the point was a frank return to the 1920s in *Gentlemen Prefer Blondes*, by Anita Loos (1888-1981). With music by Jule Styne (1905-), who composed many hits for Frank Sinatra and Dean Martin, and with assistance on the book from Joseph Fields (Lew's other son), Anita Loos adapted her own novel to the stage.

Gentlemen Prefer Blondes is the profile of an archetypal, naively opportunistic American beauty. Manipulative and greedy, Lorelei Lee comes out on top in the end. In the new spirit of character on the Broadway stage, the chorus girl finally gets the lead, and upon deeper examination she reveals herself to be—what did you expect?—a chorus girl. Carol Channing's hilarious parody of cheerful self-aggrandizement kept the show running for 740 performances.

Shirley Booth, a successful comedienne, continued to explore the American Girl, not quite as Ziegfeld had imagined, in *A Tree Grows In Brooklyn*. With book by George Abbott (1887-), lyrics by Dorothy Fields (Lew's daughter), and music by Arthur Schwartz (1900-1984), *A Tree Grows In Brooklyn* is the tale of a hapless Brooklynite who entangles herself in a series of affairs with married men, all of whom she calls "Harry" and refers to as her "husbands." Eternally optimistic, she claims "Love is the Reason." The show closed in 1951 after only 270 shows; Shirley Booth went on to play the title role in the situation comedy *Hazel*.

Robert Wright (1914-) and George Forrest (1915-), who had adapted the music of Grieg in *Song Of Norway* in 1944, established an official genre with their adaptation of *Kismet* in 1953. The theme song of *Kismet,*

Mary Martin's scrapbook from South Pacific.

"Stranger in Paradise," is based upon Alexander Borodin's *Polovtsian Dances.*

Wright and Forrest used a large portion of Borodin's catalog, and set to it the story of Arabian Nights by way of a 1911 play called *Kismet,* by Edward Knoblock. The production of *Kismet* cost an unprecedented $400,000.

Top: The 1992 revival of Guys and Dolls *marked the emergence of a brand-new Broadway star: Faith Prince, who starred as Miss Adelaide. Above: Alvin Colt's pinstripe design for Nathan Detroit in* Guys and Dolls, *1950.*

A Damon Runyon story called "The Idyll of Sarah Brown" was the basis of Frank Loesser and Abe Burrows' *Guys and Dolls,* which opened for a run of twelve hundred performances in 1950. With a cast of low-life gamblers struggling to keep "The Oldest Established Permanent Floating Crap Game in New York" alive, a chorus girl from the Hot Box Club, and a mission bandleader struggling to save all their souls,

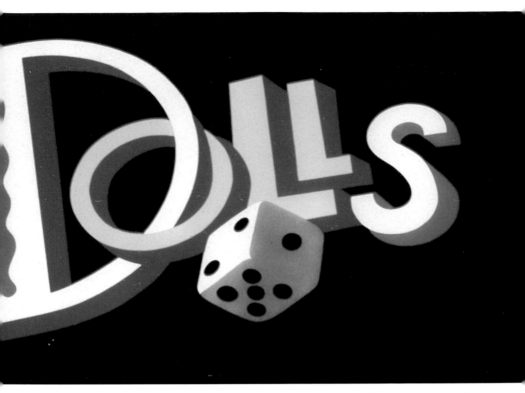

Guys and Dolls is a study in opposites unwittingly searching for common ground. When big-time Chicago gambler Sky Masterson rolls into town, all bets on these parallel worlds remaining separate are off.

Loesser musically illustrated the convergence of these worlds with his use of jazzy, syncopated Tin Pan Alley tunes for the gamblers and Hot Box Girls ("Luck be a Lady," "A Bushel and a Peck"), and strict, hymnlike marches sung in unison for the mission band. The opening numbers—"Fugue for Tin Horns," sung by the gamblers as they read off their racing forms, and "Follow the Fold," played by the mission band—establish the contrast from the beginning. But the musical styles begin to merge when Sky Masterson's plan to win a bet by dating Sarah Brown, the mission bandleader, goes awry and

Frank Loesser (1910-1969), the most happy guy.

love rears its head. "Sit Down You're Rockin' the Boat," a confessional revival song, is sung by the entire cast in a mission meeting that Masterson forces the gamblers to attend.

The oldest established permanent floating crap game in New York. The gamblers sing "Luck Be a Lady" below the streets of the city.

Although his father was a piano teacher, Loesser wrote only lyrics for the first part of his career, collaborating in Hollywood with such popular songwriters as Hoagy Carmichael and Johnny Mercer. He rose to become the music director at several studios, and wrote many popular hits, including "Jingle, Jangle, Jingle." During the war he began composing his own music, and his earliest attempt, "Praise the Lord and Pass the Ammunition," sold over two million copies in 1942. He also wrote "On a Slow Boat to China" and "Baby It's Cold Outside" for Hollywood. *Guys and Dolls* was his second attempt on Broadway, after *Where's Charley?* in 1948.

Guys and Dolls was Abe Burrows' Broadway debut. The book was originally written by Jo Swerling, who had worked in Hollywood with the Marx Brothers. In fact, Burrows had also worked with Cole Porter (Can Can, 1953, and Silk Stockings, 1955). But as problems arose, Burrows was called in to rewrite the script. The Loesser-Burrows team would go on to win a Pulitzer Prize for How to Succeed in Business Without Really Trying in 1961.

Frank Loesser devoted the years after Guys and Dolls to his labor of love, The Most Happy Fella, which opened on Broadway in 1956. Adapting Frank Howard's novel They Knew What They Wanted, Loesser wrote the music, lyrics, and book, pouring himself into the tale of an Italian-American vineyard owner in

California who falls in love at first sight. Starring a singer from the Metropolitan Opera, Robert Weede, *The Most Happy Fella* reveled in the Italian operatic tradition, with little dialogue and lots of exuberant song. But like *Guys and Dolls*, *The Most Happy Fella* explored musical contrasts and produced several popular hits: "Standin' on the Corner," "Big-D, Little-A, Double-L, A-S," and a ballad, "Joey, Joey." In demonstration of the love that grows between the late-middle-aged Tony and the waitress of his dreams, whom he woos through the mail, Loesser's score integrates two distinct musical genres, lending the best of each to the other.

The interplay of musical styles not only paralleled the progression of plot, but also established a vivid and lively cultural contrast in characterization, from the zany "Abbodanza," sung by delirious Italian vineyard workers, to the snappy, relaxed, all-American "Standin' on the Corner," tossed off by a displaced Texan and his cronies. With a run of 676 performances, *The Most Happy Fella* was by all accounts a hit (despite the fact that Broadway was overshadowed that season by *My Fair Lady*).

The Pajama Game was the smash hit of 1954. George Abbott wrote the book with Richard Bissell, based on the latter's novel *7 and ½ Cents*; the music and lyrics were by Richard Adler (1921-) and Terry Ross; and the choreography was by Bob Fosse. *The Pajama Game* was the dramatization of a labor dispute in a garment factory over a pay raise of 7 ½ cents. The plot revolves around a union leader who falls in love with a member of management; the blue-collar setting was refreshing for Broadway. Starring Carol Harrey and John Raitt, father of blues artist Bonnie Raitt, *The Pajama Game* ran for 1,063 performances and was filmed in 1957, with Doris Day and Rock Hudson in the lead roles.

As a sad, sweet elegy, Sigmund Romberg's *The Girl In the Pink Tights* appeared on Broadway three years after his death. Romberg chose to fictionalize the story of the Parisian ballet company that appeared in *The Black Crook* by creating a romance between the playwright and a ballerina. Joseph Fields and Jerome Chorodov worked together to reconstruct the book after Romberg died. The reworked show didn't play well in 1954—it ran for only 115 shows—but it endures as a poignant footnote to a dedicated artist.

But Romberg's wasn't the only show playing poorly in 1954. *The House Of Flowers,* a collaborative effort by Harold Arlen, the jazz master of Broadway, and Truman Capote (1924–1984), a member of the literary avant garde, also fared

Workers united by Bob Fosse's choreography in The Pajama Game, *1992.*

American Operetta Composers

Sheet music for Victor Herbert's "Ah! Sweet Mystery of Life."

Of the three most influential American operetta composers—Victor Herbert (1859–1924), Rudolf Friml (1879–1972), and Sigmund Romberg—Victor Herbert was the most successful, both artistically and commercially. Herbert's *Babes In Toyland* (1903) is one of the few American operettas considered to be a classic. Herbert was accessible to U.S. audiences because his approach incorporated a wide variety of styles.

An Irish-born cellist trained in Vienna, Herbert came to America in 1886 to work for the orchestra of the Metropolitan Opera. His scores were a pastiche of European musical traditions: German art song intermingled with Irish ballads and Viennese waltzes. Herbert also occasionally used ragtime rhythms, but never convincingly. While he was able to choose the ingredients of Americana better than other composers, Herbert cooked at the wrong temperature to make truly indigenous works.

Rudolf Friml was a Czech pianist who had studied under Dvořák at the conservatory in Prague. His first operetta, *The Firefly*, was a success in 1912 and is still performed today by light opera companies. He went on to compose about twenty works, but due to his rigorous training, he was incapable of continuing in the kind of voice that American musicals ultimately developed.

Sigmund Romberg was perhaps the least talented but surely the most persistent of the three. Born in Hungary in 1887, Romberg originally set out to become an engineer. While in college in Vienna, however, he discovered the theater, and moved to New York at twenty-two. He worked as a restaurant pianist until he got his big break writing scores for Al Jolson. He went on to work for Florenz Ziegfeld before staging his own shows.

Rudolf Friml.

The Student Prince, *a classic American operetta, 1924.*

His first true hit, *Blossom Time* (1921), was actually his thirteenth production. *Blossom Time* was a fictitious biography of Franz Schubert, set to the subject's own music. Romberg was a specialist in adapting symphonic music to the operetta form, with a particular fondness for Romantic composers.

He owned an enormous library of musical scores, which he spent hours poring over.

Romberg's best-known works are *The Student Prince* (1924) and *The Desert Song* (1926), on which he collaborated with Oscar Hammerstein II.

Gwen Verdon with Tab Hunter in the 1958 Warner Brothers film version of Damn Yankees.

poorly on Broadway. An effort perhaps flawed by the fact that Capote was in Switzerland and Arlen was in the United States at the time, *The House Of Flowers* had only a short run. Starring Diahann Carroll, it was the story of a young girl living in a Caribbean brothel—an idea that predates the Brooke Shields film *Pretty Baby* by some twenty-five years.

Adler and Ross returned to Broadway in 1955 with *Damn Yankees*. Based on the novel *The Year the Yankees Won the Pennant*, by Douglas Wissell, *Damn Yankees* is the story of a man who sells his soul to the devil to play baseball with the winning team in a pennant race against the Yankees. With George Abbott's book and direction, and Bob Fosse's choreography, *Damn Yankees* was destined to hit a homer; Gwen Verdon's appearance in a supporting role, however, snagged a grand slam of 1,019 performances for the show. The quintessential Fosse dancer—she was Fosse's wife—Gwen Verdon had caught the public eye with her performance in the Adam and Eve ballet in *Can Can* in 1953. But she had never attempted an integrated acting, dancing, and singing role. Playing Lola, the devil's assistant (sent into the locker room to seduce the hero), Verdon stopped the show with her number "Whatever Lola Wants (Lola Gets)."

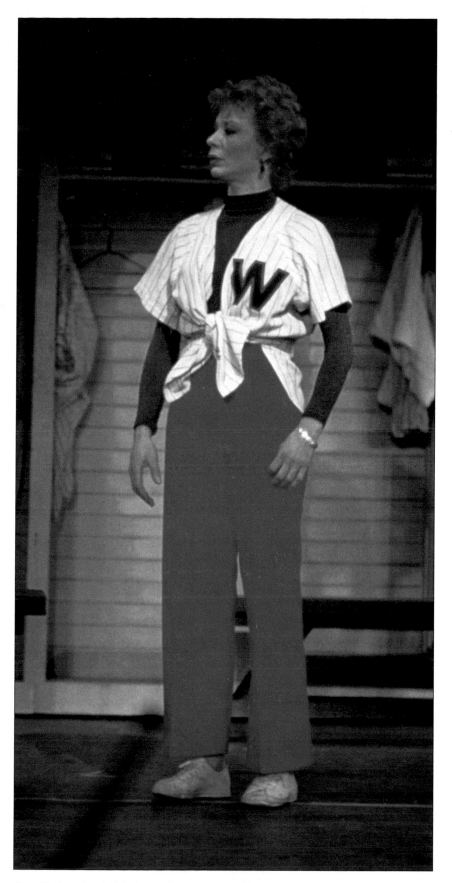

Gwen Verdon epitomized the hot, modern dance style of Broadway in the 1950s.

Theater Technology

Technological advances are always put to ingenious use in the theater, but the effect of technology on the relationship between theater and audience has never again been so dramatic and immediate as in the first part of the twentieth century.

Coinciding with the smash hit *No, No, Nanette!* in 1925, the mass production of the gramophone gave the public endless access to Vincent Youman's "Tea for Two" and "I Want to Be Happy," perhaps sounding the death knell for musicals of the 1920s.

Rudy Vallee

Rudy Vallee, a Yale crooner, began broadcasting *Variety* in 1933. When he sang "Smoke Gets in Your Eyes," the stage show *Roberta* sold out overnight. His band, the Connecticut Yankees, was named for Rodgers and Hart's 1927 show, *A Connecticut Yankee in King Arthur's Court.*

When performing live, Vallee would use a collegiate megaphone to augment his intimate, untrained voice. This use of a megaphone represented the point at which popular and Broadway music began to diverge. Songs written to hit the back wall of a Broadway theater didn't transpose well into the newer, more intimate sound coming over the radio.

The contrast between acoustic and amplified vocal performance also accounts for the sharp difference between Broadway and Hollywood musicals. Hollywood musicals are a genre unto themselves, a different medium. The song "Diamonds Are A Girl's Best Friend" from *Gentlemen Prefer Blondes,* is associated inextricably with Marilyn Monroe's performance in the 1953 film, so much so that remembering the character's name (Lorelei Lee) is a strain. Carol Channing's performance in the 1949 Broadway production is broader and richer than Monroe's, but could never work on screen. Likewise, Monroe's delicate breathlessness wouldn't have reached the second row in a theater (no matter how small).

Broadway stars have rarely been allowed to re-create their roles for the screen. Julie Andrews is an exception, but even she was replaced by Audrey Hepburn in the film of *My Fair Lady.* Of course, Julie Andrews herself replaced Mary Martin in the film version of *The Sound of Music.*

In the movie version of Gentlemen Prefer Blondes, *Marilyn Monroe and Jane Russell make it difficult for a gentleman to be sure.*

Sheet music for "With a Little Bit of Luck" from the original production of My Fair Lady.

Alan Jay Lerner (1918–1986) and Frederick Loewe (1901–1988) hit it really big with *My Fair Lady.* Based on *Pygmalion,* by George Bernard Shaw (1856–1950), *My Fair Lady* took a peek at the separation of the classes (safely demonstrated in a British milieu). Lavishly staged with sets by Oliver Smith and costumes by Cecil Beaton, the show ran for 2,717 performances. When it went to London, a countdown to the day of its opening was published in the daily papers.

My Fair Lady was not so much a hit show as a cultural phenomenon. Frederick Loewe and Alan Lerner had already produced two hits with *Brigadoon* in 1947 and *Paint Your Wagon* in 1951, but this lavish production took Lerner and Loewe permanently into the firmament of Broadway stardom. The catalog of the show is perhaps the most familiar of all Broadway musicals: "I've Grown Accustomed to Her Face," "Wouldn't it Be Loverly," "With a Little Bit of Luck," "Get

A page from Lerner and Loewe's original score to My Fair Lady, 1955.

Me to the Church on Time," "On the Street Where You Live," and "I Could Have Danced All Night."

My Fair Lady used the relationship between speech and song to portray the separation of the classes. Rex Harrison's distinctive talking/singing voice was the perfect instrument to convey the frustrated rigidity of social appearance, and its contrast to Julie Andrews' clear soprano musically upheld the wide breech that separates Eliza Doolittle and Henry Higgins. Lerner and Loewe's presentation of Pygmalion as a musical resulted in the play being more about Higgins learning to sing than about Eliza learning to speak properly; that Higgins can never sing properly only highlights the differences between artistic and practical expression.

Meredith Willson's The Music Man beat out Leonard Bernstein's West Side Story for the Best Play and Best Composer Tony Awards in 1957. Writing his first

Broadway show at the age of fifty-five, Willson capped off a performance career that had run the gamut from principal flutist for John Phillip Sousa's band and for the New York Philharmonic to a stint as a popular radio conductor. Rather than a mix of musical genres, *The Music Man* was more a celebration of the myriad uses and expressions of plain, popular, middle-American musical styles: the march, the barbershop quartet, and the waltz. With firsthand Sousa inspiration, Willson's rousing "Seventy-Six Trombones" infused the ordinary with an excitement that kept rolling for 1,375 performances. Robert Preston, in his first singing role, used his non-

Barbara Cook and Robert Preston as Marion and Harold in Meredith Willson's The Music Man, *1957.*

singing voice to its best advantage—a ploy no doubt made possible by Rex Harrison's performance the previous year. Harold Hill, a salesman trying to con a town into buying nonexistent band equipment, is himself incited to sincerity by the unswerving insistence of the music itself. The rattling sales pitch of "Trouble" and bamboozle of "Seventy-Six Trombones" are gradually overcome by the trusting simplicity of "Wells Fargo Wagon" and the poignancy of Marion the Librarian's "Good Night My Someone." ("Seventy-Six Trombones" and "Good Night My Someone" are the same melody played in different tempos, the musical mirror of Marion and Harold's attraction of opposites.)

Betty Comden (1919–) and Adolph Green (1915–), a team probably best known for writing the 1952 film *Singin' In The Rain*, hooked up with Jule Styne to produce *Bells Are Ringing*. With choreography by Jerome Robbins and Bob Fosse, this show ran for 924 performances. The story of a telephone message operator

Robert Preston was the third choice for the role of Harold Hill, behind Gene Kelly and Danny Kaye. Unable to sing or dance, he nevertheless proved he could charm a Broadway audience.

who falls for a playwright client was a Comden and Green original. *Bells Are Ringing* was an imaginative combination of screwball comedy and backstage romance. "Just in Time" and "The Party's Over" were both hits from the show.

Although based on the autobiography of burlesque queen Gypsy Rose Lee, *Gypsy* was more the story of her willful and domineering mother. Mama Rose's vain attempts to launch Gypsy's sister June to the top of the burlesque world finally leave Gypsy neglected. June bitterly disappoints her mother by running away with a chorus boy and abandoning the business; Merman's number "Everything's Coming Up Roses" was a bravura exhibition of Mama Rose's inability to see anything but the shiniest surfaces of show business.

Jule Styne, who wrote the music for *Gypsy*, had a talent for writing for

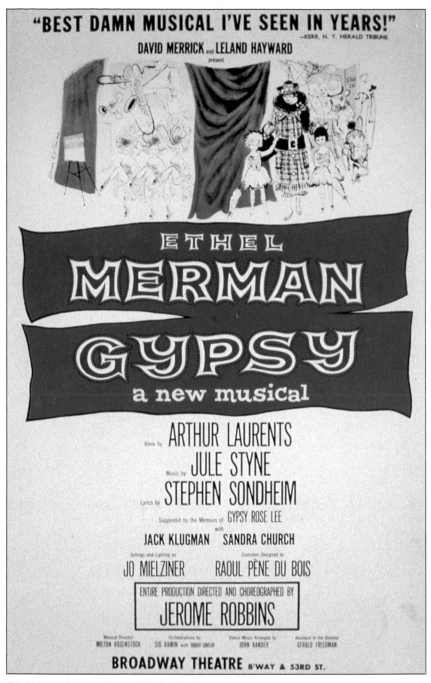

"BEST DAMN MUSICAL I'VE SEEN IN YEARS!"
—KERR, N. Y. HERALD TRIBUNE

DAVID MERRICK and LELAND HAYWARD
present

ETHEL
MERMAN
GYPSY
a new musical

Book by ARTHUR LAURENTS
Music by JULE STYNE
Lyrics by STEPHEN SONDHEIM
Suggested by the Memoirs of GYPSY ROSE LEE
with
JACK KLUGMAN   SANDRA CHURCH
Settings and Lighting by   Costumes Designed by
JO MIELZINER   RAOUL PÈNE DU BOIS
ENTIRE PRODUCTION DIRECTED AND CHOREOGRAPHED BY
JEROME ROBBINS
Musical Director   Orchestrations by   Dance Music Arranged by   Assistant to the Director
MILTON ROSENSTOCK   SID RAMIN with ROBERT GINZLER   JOHN KANDER   GERALD FREEDMAN

BROADWAY THEATRE B'WAY & 53RD ST.

Ethel Merman's name alone could sell out the house.

particular performers. The composer of many Frank Sinatra hits, Styne also composed specifically for Mary Martin, Judy Holliday, Carol Channing, and Barbra Streisand. The very talented Styne had a thriving career writing for Hollywood and the popular music business (teamed with lyricist Sammy Cahn) before turning to Broadway. More known for his swank swing style ("Just in Time"), Styne let out all the stops for *Gypsy*. From June's slithery little-girlish "Let Me Entertain You" to Mama Rose's crushing final number, "Rose's Turn," Styne produced the definitive Broadway sound.

From Puerto Rico to Hell's Kitchen to Broadway: "I Like to Be in America," from West Side Story, 1957.

Stephen Sondheim and Arthur Laurents debuted on Broadway at the top when they collaborated (as lyricist and book writer, respectively) with Leonard Bernstein on *West Side Story* in 1957. *Gypsy* was the second Broadway project for both of them. Also participating in both projects was Jerome Robbins. It was Robbins who had suggested to Bernstein the idea of transposing the story of Shakespeare's *Romeo and Juliet* to Hell's Kitchen; and Robbins' direction and choreography on both shows were essential elements of their successes.

Rodgers and Hammerstein's final collaboration, *The Sound of Music*, opened on Broadway in 1959. Like *Gypsy*, *The Sound of Music* is based on a true story, but this is where any likeness between the two musicals ends. *The Sound of Music* is the story of Maria, an Austrian postulant who helps the von Trapp family elude the Nazis (and who eventually becomes a von Trapp herself). Julie Andrews is most familiar as the star of the 1965 film version of the musical, but Mary Martin—the quintessential Rodgers and Hammerstein star—originated the role on Broadway. Although its plot centers on European concerns, the show's foundation in reality and its focus on aesthetic freedom in the face of oppression fostered its great appeal to Broadway audiences.

Shows about show business are a favorite Broadway formula. Not only do they provide ready-made drama—the foibles and fables of trying to go on with (or get into) the show—but they also offer ample opportunity for big, glitzy, irrelevant production numbers that won't hinder the main plot in any way. They usually consist of two plots—the "onstage" plot and the "backstage" plot.

In the 1950s, the backstage plot moved onstage, and the energy formerly expended on sideshow glamor was redirected to explore the nooks and crannies of everyday life. Garment workers, flower sellers, gamblers, baseball fans, and Brooklyn bachelorettes became the stars of the show. Broadway itself became the onstage production number for the backstage plot of society at large.

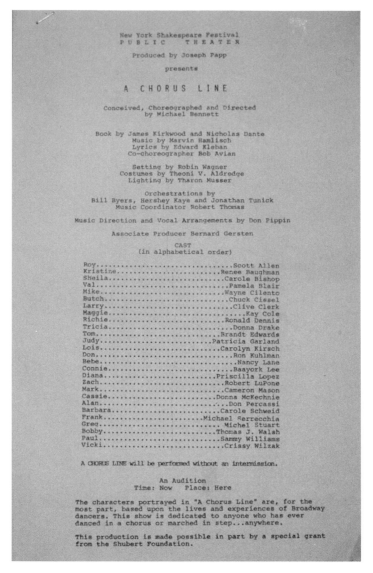

A *Chorus Line* is the ultimate backstage play. Both a revue and a book musical, the onstage plot and the backstage plot are the same: individual characters step forward to tell their stories as they audition for roles in a Broadway chorus. The chorus line reveals what is most important to each of them, what most drives their yearning for a spot on the line. The dual plots are resolved in "One," as splashy a production number as ever graced the Broadway stage.

The thrill of "One" springs from participating in the realization of the characters' dreams, and from the intimacy of knowing their lives are not so different from our own. In much the same way, the Broadway story has great appeal because it is the story of an entire nation told in a way that sweeps up the audience with its relentless enthusiasm.

The plot and setting of A Chorus Line—*an audition on a bare stage—paralleled its rise from a modest, Off-Broadway production in 1975 (program above) to the longest-running hit in the history of Broadway. It won a Pulitzer Prize in 1976, and swept both the Obie and Tony awards.*

A Short Glossary of Terms About the Broadway Musical

Book: The spoken dialogue.

Book Musical: A play integrated with a musical score that contributes to the development of plot and character.

Choreography: The composition and arrangement of dance.

Libretto: From Latin *libre* ("book"), the words that accompany a musical piece.

Light opera: British operettas, with the emphasis on parody and wit in the libretto, rather than upon the music.

Lyrics: The words of the songs.

Musical Comedy: A revue consisting of music interspersed with comic skits and sketches.

Opéra bouffe: Before the mid-eighteenth century, French vaudeville. After Offenbach's *Orpheus In The Underworld* (1859), the forerunner of operetta.

Opera buffa: Seventeenth-century Italian popular opera; light, comic plots incorporating dialogue sung in a style called *recitative*.

Opéra comique: The French version of *opera buffa*–dialogue is spoken, not sung.

Operetta: A style originating in Vienna, with scores that lean toward waltzes and marches and require trained voices to sing.

Score: The music, including orchestration and voice.

Photography and Illustration Credits

© Evan Agostini, pp. 8, 9 top, 48-49, 52 top; Archive Photos, pp. 9 bottom, 56; ©Walter Weissman/Envision,p. 14 top ;FPG International, pp. 10 left, 23 top, 25, 42 top, 44; Courtesy of the Metropolitan Opera Archives, pp. 10-11, 12-13; Courtesy of the Museum of the City of New York/The Theater Collection; pp. 11 bottom, 12 bottom, 13 bottom, 15, 16, 17, 18, 19, 20-21, 22, 23 bottom, 24, 26 all, 27, 28 both, 29, 30 both, 31, 32-33, 34, 35, 36, 37, 38 bottom, 38-39, 39 bottom, 40-41, 42 bottom, 43, 44, 46, 47, 48 bottom, 49 bottom, 50-51, 52-53, 54-55, 57, 61, 62-63, 64, 65, 66, © Motion Picture and Television Photo Archive, p. 58 both.

For Further Reading...

●● Astaire, Fred *Steps in Time*. New York: Harper, 1959.

●● Bordman, Gerald *The American Musical Theatre*. New York: Oxford University Press, 1978.

●● Eells, George *Cole Porter: The Life That Late He Led*. New York: Putnam, 1967.

●● Gershwin, Ira *Lyrics on Several Occasions*. New York: Knopf, 1959.

●● Green, Stanley *Encyclopedia of the Musical Theater*. New York: Oxford University Press, 1974.

●● Hart, Dorothy *Thou Swell, Thou Witty: The Life and Lyrics of Lorenz Hart*, Harper & Row.

●● Jablonski, Edward and Lawrence D. Stewart *The Gershwin Years*. New York: Doubleday, 1973.

●● Jackson, Arthur *The Book of Musicals*. Crown Publishers: New York 1977.

●● Kreuger, Miles *Showboat: The Story of a Classic American Musical*. New York: Oxford University Press.

●● Lauffe, Abe *Broadway's Greatest Musicals*. New York: Funk & Wagnall's, 1977.

●● Lerner, Alan Jay *On the Street Where I Live*. New York: Norton, 1978.

●● Lerner, Alan Jay *The Musical Theater: A Celebration*. New York: McGraw-Hill, 1986

●● Marx, Samuel, and Jan Clayton *Rodgers and Hart*. Putnam.

●● Mast, Gerald *Can't Help Singin': The American Musical on Stage and Screen*. Woodstock, New York: The Overlook Press, 1987.

●● Mordden, Ethan *Broadway Babies: The People Who Made the American Musical*. New York: Oxford University Press, 1983.

●● Rodgers, Richard *Musical Stages: An Autobiography*. New York: Random House, 1975.

●● Toll, Robert *Blacking Up: The Minstrel Show in Nineteenth Century America*. New York: Oxford University Press, 1974.

●● Wilder, Alec *American Popular Song: The Great Innovators 1900-1950*. New York: Oxford University Press, 1972.

●● Wodehouse, P.G., and Guy Bolton *Bring on the Girls!* New York: Simon and Schuster, 1953.

Listener's Guide to the Broadway Musical

George and Ira Gershwin:

From *Girl Crazy*: Embraceable You; But Not for Me; I Got Rhythm; Sam and Delilah

From *Funny Face*: 'S Wonderful; My One and Only

From *Of Thee I Sing*: Wintergreen for President; Some Girls Can Bake a Pie; Jilted; Who Cares?

From *Porgy and Bess*: Summertime; I Got Plenty of Nothin'; It Ain't Necessarily So

Marvin Hamlisch and Edward Kleban:

From *A Chorus Line*: At The Ballet; Dance: Ten, Looks: Three; One; What I Did For Love

Jim Jacobs and Warren Casey:

From *Grease*: Summer Nights; Freddy, My Love; We Go Together; Beauty School Dropout

Jerome Kern:

From *Sally*: Look for the Silver Lining

From *Swing Time*: The Way You Look Tonight; Pick Youself Up; A Fine Romance

From *Roberta*: Smoke Gets in Your Eyes; Yesterdays

Frank Loesser:

From *Guys and Dolls*: Fugue for Tinhorns; The Oldest Established; Guys and Dolls; Luck Be A Lady; Sue Me

From *The Most Happy Fella*: Abbodanza; Sposalizio; Joey, Joey; Big D

Cole Porter:

From *Anything Goes*: You're the Tops; I Get a Kick Out of You; Blow, Gabriel, Blow; Anything Goes

From *Kiss Me Kate*: Another Op'nin', Another Show; Wunderbar; We Open in Venice; Tom, Dick or Harry; I Hate Men; Too Darn Hot; Always True to You (In My Fashion); Brush Up Your Shakespeare

Richard Rodgers and Lorenz Hart:

From *A Connecticut Yankee in King Arthur's Court*: Thou Swell; To Keep My Love Alive; My Heart Stood Still

From *Babes in Arms*: My Funny Valentine; Johnny One Note

From *On Your Toes*: There's A Small Hotel; Too Good for the Average Man; Glad to Be Unhappy; It's Got to be Love

From *Jumbo*: My Romance

From *Pal Joey*: Plant You Now, Dig You Later; Red Hot Mama; You Mustn't Kick it Around; Our Little Den of Iniquity; Zip; I Could Write a Book

Steven Schwartz:

From *The Magic Show*: Lion Tamer; Two's Company; West End Avenue

Stephen Sondheim:

From *A Funny Thing Happened on the Way to the Forum*: Comedy Tonight

From *A Little Night Music*: Send in the Clowns

Jule Styne:

From *Bells are Ringing*: On My Own; Just in Time; The Party's Over

Harry Tierney and Joseph McCarthy:

From *Irene*: Alice Blue Gown; Irene

Vincent Youmans:

From *No, No, Nanette!*: I Want to Be Happy; No, No, Nanette; Tea for Two; Take a Little One-Step

Index